Baby fun

ANNE KNECHT-BOYER

CARROLL & BROWN PUBLISHERS LIMITED

This edition first published in 2006
in the United Kingdom by

Carroll & Brown Publishers Limited
20 Lonsdale Road, London NW6 6RD

Editors Tom Broder, Virginia Sheridan
Photography Jules Selmes, Trish Gant
Production Karol Davies, Nigel Reed
Computer support Paul Stradling, Nicky Rein

Text © 2006 Anne Knecht-Boyer
Illustrations and compilation © 2006
Carroll & Brown Limited, London

A CIP catalogue record for this book is available from
the British Library

ISBN 1-904760-43-0
ISBN-13 978-1-904760-43-6

The moral right of Anne Knecht-Boyer to be identified
as the author of this work has been asserted in
accordance with the Copyright, Designs and Patents
Act of 1988

Visit the website at: www.pekip.com.hk

Reproduced by RALI, Spain
Printed and bound in Spain by Bookprint

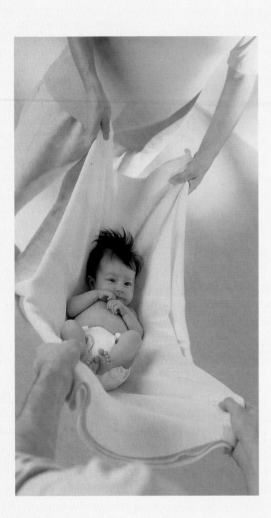

contents

introduction

Many of the parents in my classes ask me what toys they can buy to make their children smarter. Are black-and-white patterns effective? Can Mozart music tapes really raise a baby's IQ? Are interactive electronic toys worth the expense? I tell them that they already have the most effective, stimulating, and responsive plaything available for their babies – and they can find it by looking in a mirror.

Parents and caregivers – humans rather than inanimate objects – are the best and most effective early playmates for infants. We can provide language training and physical exercise for our little ones, as well as hours of amusement with actions as simple as the opening and closing of a hand. We can laugh and sing with, react to, love, and hug our babies in ways that even the most technically sophisticated toy cannot. Through simple, unpressurized play, we can help our infants develop healthy emotional, physical, intellectual and psychosocial skills.

The only problem is that many of us have forgotten how to play. We are so concerned with all the "to dos" of infant-rearing – nappy-changing, feeding, bathing, scheduling doctor's visits, establishing good sleep patterns – that we sometimes forget to interact with our children playfully. This book is, in part, about discovering how to play with infants. But it is also about giving structure to that play by incorporating activities that stimulate particular motor skills at the appropriate stage of development.

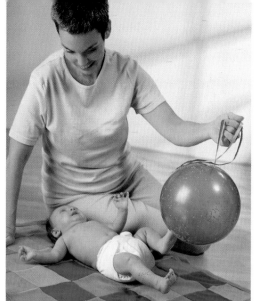

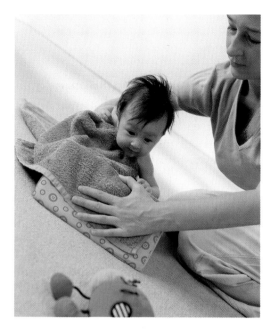

The PEKiP programme

The exercises in this book are based on the Prague Parent-Infant Programme or PEKiP (Prager Eltern Kind Programm). This programme developed from the observations of Prague psychiatrist Jaroslav Koch (who studied mother-child interactions at his Institute of Mother and Child Care), as well as the input of research professors, paediatric nurses, social workers and, of course, parents. Although the programme's aim, "to accompany and support parents and babies during the sensitive first-year bonding process," may sound modern, the first PEKiP course was taught more than 25 years ago.

I am a certified PEKiP instructor, but my first introduction to the programme was as a new mother. Because I had trained as a psychomotor skills therapist, when my daughter, Anne-Catherine, was three months old, I looked for a structured class for her. I was instantly impressed with the PEKiP methodology. The results were stunning, too. My daughter became more playful at home – indeed, she seemed to initiate and anticipate playtime with me – and her gross and fine motor skills and social and cognitive abilities developed rapidly. Most importantly, the PEKiP programme was flexible enough to allow her to learn and explore at her own pace, with me as her guide.

When I moved to Hong Kong, a place with no PEKiP classes, I realized that I would not have the same opportunities with my son, Lukas. This was the impetus I needed to train as an instructor. In six years of leading PEKiP classes, I have had the satisfaction of facilitating the bonding process between over a thousand parents and children and of watching those infants move confidently through their developmental stages.

what is sensory integration?

During the first year of life, your young baby is bombarded with new sensory experiences: the bark of a dog, the coolness of a tile floor, or the warmth of sunlight through a window. As your child grows older he continues to experience new sensations. The process by which his brain learns to organize and interpret these different sensory experiences is called sensory integration (SI). This process begins in the womb when a baby senses his mother's movements. As he grows older, new sensory experiences require him to integrate ever greater amounts of information. The ability to organize sensations from within his own body and integrate them with those from his surrounding environment, allows your baby to use his body efficiently and effectively within this environment.

Sensory integration provides a crucial foundation for the more complex learning skills needed later in life. It plays a vital role in your baby's rapidly developing motor skills, allowing him to move his body proficiently. It also is critical to his ability to access learning, and helps in the development of good social skills, attention and emotional stability.

The concept of SI was developed by Jean Ayres, PhD, an occupational therapist. She researched the ways in which sensory processing and motor planning disorders interfere with daily life and function. She saw that children with SI problems become slow learners or develop behavioural problems. Her work was taken up by other therapists and specialists in the field..

Sense and movement
Your baby is not a passive recipient of sensory information. In the first year or so of life, your child learns to explore himself and the world

around him by the use of his senses and movement. A baby playing with toys will typically touch, throw and kick them; hide and retrieve them; or push, pull and shake them. As he does this, he listens to the sounds they make and watches what happens to them. Through these multiple sensory-motor means he becomes familiar with the world outside himself and learns to achieve some mastery over it.

Four distinct groups of skills develop during this phase, the mastery of which constitute your child's first steps toward independence and form the basis of his ability to learn about his environment:

1 He learns to recognize many features of his environment.
2 He becomes aware of himself as distinct from his environment.
3 He learns to change his body position and move in space.

YOUR BABY'S HIDDEN SENSES

Most of us are familiar with a baby's basic senses — taste, touch, smell, sight and sound — but movement, the pull of gravity and his body's position in space are also sensory experiences. These sensations are detected by two less well-known sensory systems — the vestibular and proprioceptive.

• The vestibular system involves the structures within the inner ear. When your baby's head changes position, fluid in his inner ear sends information to his brain, which tells his body that it is off balance, in motion, or higher off the ground than normal. This system develops early *in utero*, and through its many connections with the rest of the brain is believed to provide the foundation for functions including bilateral coordination (the ability of the body to use both sides in a coordinated manner) and lateralization (the specialization of each side of the body).

• The proprioceptive system provides feedback from the muscles, joints and tendons, and helps with your baby's awareness of his position in space. If there is a disturbance in the proprioceptive system, a child may be clumsy, fall, seem to maintain abnormal body postures, have difficulty manipulating small objects and may resist trying different types of movement.

4 He learns to grasp, hold, release and manipulate objects at will.
The stimulating activities in this book will help your child master these skills through the effective integration of his senses.

comforting holds
in safe hands

Holding and transporting your baby is an art. Done correctly, it is one of the best ways to make her feel loved and secure. Despite what anyone else might say, carrying your baby will not spoil her – at this age, she wants and needs to be carried and rocked. These sensations make your baby happy!

This kind of gentle sensory stimulation will provide a good foundation for later sensory-motor development. The motion stimulates your baby's vestibular system (inner ear) providing a regulating effect on her overall physiology and motor development. It also encourages her to use certain muscle groups, such as those that help her to lift her head. You still should be very careful to support her head as you lift her; her muscles are not yet strong enough to hold her head up unassisted.

All newborns love being cradled in your arms and older babies enjoy the more "grown-up"

hip hold (see below). Both these holds are good for baby and for you. On the right are a few more holds that will allow you and your baby to use different muscle groups while still ensuring that baby is securely nestled.

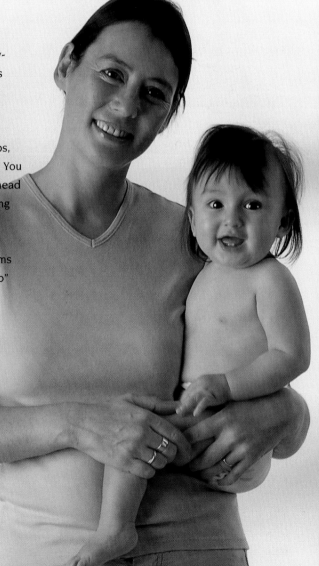

SAFETY FIRST

Changing baby's position frequently will help to strengthen her neck muscles equally on both sides. You must try to keep your own body balanced by using both shoulders, both arms, and your upper and lower back equally. This will help prevent muscle strain, especially as your baby gets heavier.

The colic clinch

Some colicky babies like this hold because it places pressure on the tummy and helps to expel gas. Many parents also appreciate this face down position because it directs baby's cries away from adult ears. Carry your baby face down with her upper body supported in the crook of your arm and her chest lying on your forearm. Baby's head should be free to move up and to the side. Place your other arm between her legs to support her lower body.

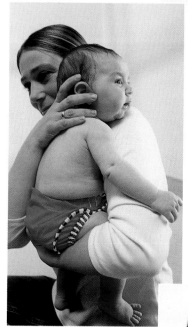

The shoulder nestle

This is a natural position for burping. Hold your baby's head against your shoulder, supporting her neck or patting her back with one hand. Cup her bottom with the other.

The seat hold (above)

This position gives your baby the freedom to focus on the sights and sounds of the world around her. It's a great posture for introducing your little one to the world. Place one arm around your baby's chest and press gently to support her weight. Use the other arm as a "bench" for baby's bottom to sit on.

The snuggle position

This is one of the most popular positions for mothers and other caregivers. Snuggle your baby against your chest. Use one arm to support your baby's lower body and put your other arm on his back. Let his head be free to look around above your shoulder. Make sure, however, that you don't carry your baby on one side only, as this can lead to muscle strain.

exercises for you, fun for your baby

Young babies require a great deal of love and attention, not to mention hard work, and it can be difficult to find the time to get back into shape after pregnancy. Adapting your exercise routine to involve your baby can give the best of both worlds: you get the chance to get fit, or at least work on your back and stomach muscles; your baby gets to play a fun, stimulating game with his mother.

A young baby makes the ideal fitness aid – his growth keeps pace with your return to fitness – and he will enjoy the experience as much as you. As well as helping you to tone, activities such as rocking and carrying stimulate your baby, encouraging healthy physiological and motor development and helping his breathing and growth.

Like the activities in the main programme, it is best to wait until your baby is six weeks old before beginning these exercises. They should be an extension of regular play – so make sure you both enjoy them!

SAFETY FIRST

If you have had a caesarean delivery you may need to take things a little more slowly. Speak to a health professional before attempting anything too strenuous and listen to what your body tells you.

For starters...

A two- to three-month-old baby's neck muscles are still weak and you should make sure that his head is well supported. For a gentle introduction to the exercises, lie back with your knees bent and your feet on the floor. Prop your baby on your thighs, with his head resting against your knees. Keep your hands on either side of his body to stabilize his head, and rock gently from side to side.

Back and forth

Sit down cross-legged with your baby in your lap. Hold him by the chest with his back against your body. Slowly and easily, rock back and forth. This will give him an idea of space while providing a gentle workout for your stomach.

Up and down

1 Sit on the floor with your knees bent and your feet flat on the floor. Place your infant on his tummy on your lower legs, facing toward you.

2 Roll onto your back, lifting your legs up as you come back. Keeping a safe grip on your baby, use your legs to swing him up and down in the air. Lift and lower him a couple of times.

3 Using your stomach muscles, bring yourself back up into a sitting position. Go back and forth to give your stomach a good workout.

mini yoga

Young babies are naturally very supple, but they can easily lose this flexibility as they grow older. Through her first year of life, as your baby starts to move around and support her own weight, her muscles become much stronger. But as her joints and muscles develop, they also start to lose some of their natural flexibility. The simple stretches shown here will help your baby to maintain suppleness as she grows and develops, and encourage a wider range of movement.

These stretches are a useful addition to the activities in the main PEKiP programme, as they encourage your baby's sensory-motor exploration and therefore her physical development. You can start doing these exercises at six weeks, or whenever you begin the main programme of activities, and carry on doing them for as long as you and your baby enjoy them. Try to do a few stretches every morning when you sit down to play with your baby.

Begin by laying your baby down with her back along your thighs. Cross her arms at her chest, and repeat, alternating arms so that first one, then the other, crosses over the top.

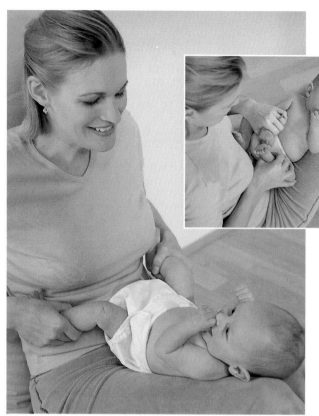

Hand to foot

Take hold of one of your baby's arms at the wrist and cross her hand over to touch her opposite foot. Tickle the sole of her foot with her fingers. Now repeat with the other hand and foot.

Bicycle

Gently push your baby's knees into her tummy, one after the other, in a slow, smooth cycling motion. This gentle knees up and down movement promotes flexible hip and knee joints and can help to relieve colic.

Good morning, little feet

Cross your baby's legs over at her tummy. Repeat this a few times, alternating legs so that first one, then the other, crosses over the top. Then take hold of your baby's ankle and bring her foot up towards her mouth, allowing the knee to bend and her leg to turn out at the hips. As you bring it up, say "Good morning, little foot". Then "wake up" the other foot in the same way. You shouldn't have any trouble bringing both feet up towards her mouth together. This will help open the hips, maintaining hip and leg flexibility.

Tickly feet

Hold your baby's feet so they are touching one another. Use the toes of one foot to tickle the sole of the other foot. Repeat on the other side.

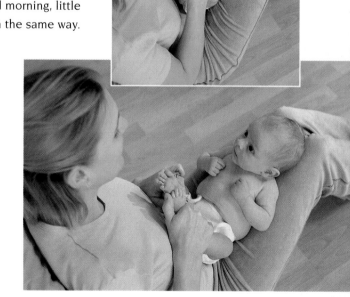

following the programme

The activities in this book are arranged by age, starting with exercises for six-week-old babies and going up to one year of age. (Before the age of six weeks you and your child probably still are recovering from the birth.) Each chapter provides a variety of stimulating activities to reinforce your infant's sensory experiences with motor skills, starting with head control and moving down the body.

You can do the activities as often as you like, but try to spend at least 10 minutes in the morning and 10 minutes in the afternoon on one-to-one play with your baby. Make sure he is ready to play and not hungry, wet, sleepy, cranky or otherwise distracted. Turn off the telephone and the television and get down to your baby's level on the floor. Talk to him and make funny faces throughout. Most importantly of all, stop playing when he has had enough – an over-stimulated baby will tire or be fussy.

Give your baby plenty of time to work out the activities – as well as being stimulating, the exercises are intended to teach your baby how to learn for himself. Let him explore at his own pace, with you as his guide, rather than rushing to help him the moment he gets stuck. This will provide him with the opportunity to develop his problem-solving skills and give him the chance to improve his strength.

If your child is not ready or able to do the activity proposed for his age, wait a week or two before trying again. The emphasis should be on stimulating, playing and bonding with your child, and certainly not on achieving targets. Every baby develops at a different rate – some babies spend a long time crawling while others skip the

crawling stage altogether, preferring to shuffle along on their bottoms. However, if you are concerned that your infant is very late in developing any sensory-motor skill, ask your healthcare professional for advice.

Consider giving your baby the chance to play nude. He will move more easily and be happier when unencumbered by bulky clothes and a nappy; if you don't believe it, try it and see the difference. He probably will urinate at some point so put a piece of plastic or a towel beneath him and have some baby wipes and paper towels on hand to clean up. Keep the room warm, comfortable and draught-free.

Above all, have fun and enjoy the miracle of your infant in his first year. He will grow up very quickly, so make the most of this very special period in his life.

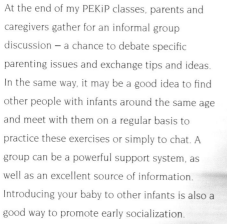

Support and socialization

At the end of my PEKiP classes, parents and caregivers gather for an informal group discussion – a chance to debate specific parenting issues and exchange tips and ideas. In the same way, it may be a good idea to find other people with infants around the same age and meet with them on a regular basis to practice these exercises or simply to chat. A group can be a powerful support system, as well as an excellent source of information. Introducing your baby to other infants is also a good way to promote early socialization.

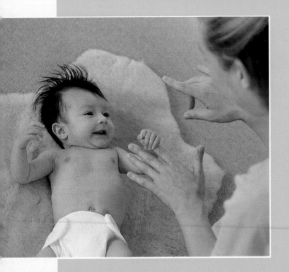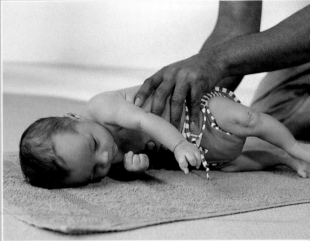

1

up to *two* months

The first six weeks of your baby's life are a time for you to get to know one another and establish a good routine. Your baby will have begun learning and absorbing new information from birth, but six weeks is the perfect time to start thinking about new, stimulating activities and challenges.

Your baby is born with a wide range of fascinating reflexes. Touch his open hand and he will tightly close his fist; touch his foot near to his toes and he will quickly curl in his toes; hold your baby with his feet touching a flat surface and he will automatically start to step. The activities in this first chapter make use of some of these natural motor reflexes to help your baby gain strength from his head to his toes.

As these reflexes gradually disappear during the first six months of life, your baby develops the ability to make voluntary movements. As early as the end of the first month, your baby may start being able to lift his own head – the

brain regions that control the head and the neck develop before those that direct the arms and legs. Your child's increasing ability to interact with his environment will encourage further progress.

The activities in this chapter make use of your child's maturing senses to stimulate further development. Your baby knows what looks, tastes, feels, sounds and smells good. He loves skin-to-skin touching. He can distinguish and respond to his mother's voice and can tell her smell from others. Talking to, singing and touching your baby will reinforce his self-esteem and comfort him. Your infant can definitely see and may choose different images to look at. He is especially interested in the human face.

All these abilities reflect the fact that even at birth your baby's sensory system is well developed. Fun, stimulating activities such as these will help him fine tune these senses, teaching him how to integrate them effectively, and encouraging his healthy physical, emotional and cognitive development.

from side to side

Young babies have impressively firm and determined grasps. This simple game uses your baby's strong grip to help her get familiar with side-to-side movement. Many babies, when they turn their heads, tend to favour one side in preference to the other. In this exercise, your baby follows your lead, so you can widen her scope to almost 180 degrees. Not only will this introduce her to movement, she will also have the opportunity to look around and discover more about her surroundings. You will help stimulate her vision, eye muscle control and motor-skill development.

Sensory integration

As your baby catches sight of and then grasps hold of your fingers, she is learning to integrate her sense of touch with her sense of vision. She also uses her vestibular system as she moves her head from side to side – her inner ear helps her to detect movement and changes in head position. These sensations of gentle body movement tend to organize your baby's brain and let her assimilate and make use of the information from her senses.

What you will need
Just you and your baby

Skills developed
Hand-eye coordination
Body perception

1 Lay your baby gently on her back and offer her the forefingers of your right and left hands to grasp. You may need to wiggle your fingers to attract her attention and let her get a visual fix on them.

2 Your baby may reach out for you herself, but you will probably need to place your fingers in her open palms – she will instinctively and tightly grab hold. Once she gets a good grasp, move your hands slowly over to one side.

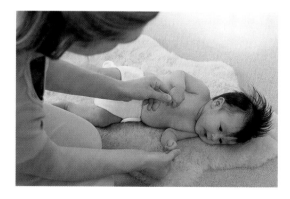

3 Observe how your baby's head turns to that side and how her little body follows her hands. Then move your fingers slowly back to the other side of her body. Eventually her hip and leg will follow too. Move her back and forth to familiarize her with the movement.

Rock-a-bye baby

To calm or quiet a fretful baby, try singing a lullaby while slowly rocking her from side to side in a blanket. The to and fro movement will gently stimulate her vestibular system, soothing and relaxing her. This activity involves two people, so it provides a chance for you and your partner to enjoy a peaceful time together with your baby.

fun with reflections

At six weeks old, your infant is just beginning to focus on objects, but his visual range is limited to about 25 cm (10 in). This is the perfect distance for presenting toys – too close or too far away from your baby's face and the object will be a frustrating blur.

Undoubtedly the most fascinating and visually interactive toy available for your baby is the human face – your baby prefers watching your face, with its full range of expressions, to any manufactured distraction, no matter how ingenious. A view of both you and your baby reflected in a mirror will both captivate and enthral him.

Sensory integration

The relationship between head control, head movement and vision is very important. Your baby's visual tracking – the ability to follow an object or person by moving his eyes and head – is dependent on his integration of these skills. His ability to track objects develops as an adaptive response to sensations from the muscles surrounding his eyes and in his neck, and sensations of gravity and movement from his inner ear. Following his reflection in the mirror will reinforce your infant's attention, focus and head control, and will help him interact with his environment.

What you will need
Medium-sized, non-breakable mirror

Skills developed
Visual tracking
Head and neck control

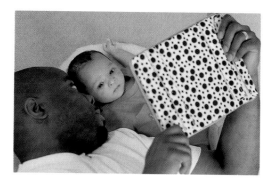

1. Place your baby down gently on his back and lie down next to him facing the ceiling. Hold the mirror above you at a distance of around 25 cm (10 in). Angle the mirror so that you are both reflected.

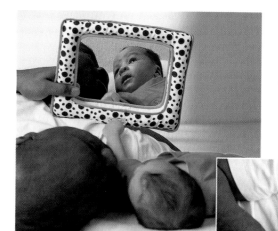

2. Allow your baby plenty of time to focus on the reflection and respond. Try changing the angle of the mirror slightly so that he can see first your reflection and then his own. Observe which face he watches more intently.

3. Move the mirror from side to side and then slowly up and down. This will encourage your baby to move, turn and even lift his head as he tries to keep the reflection in his sight.

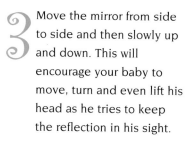

How does your baby grow?

Your child will be fascinated by the beautiful baby in the mirror but, aged two months, she will not yet recognize it as her own reflection. It is not until 15 months to two years of age – around the time she learns to say "I", "my", and "mine" – that she will be able to identify herself properly. But at two months the moving image will still intrigue her and may provide a good way to soothe her when she is crying.

bottom down, head up

Your infant's posture and strength affect what she can do for herself and the use she can make of her environment. This activity teaches your baby to stretch her legs out from underneath her and increase her head and neck control. At six weeks, if you place your baby in the prone position she will look like a little frog: her weight is shifted onto her upper extremities, her hips are flexed and her pelvis is elevated. Eventually she will learn to shift her weight back, pushing her bottom down as she lifts her head. For now, though, you can help her by placing a rolled-up towel or a foam wedge under her chest.

The exercise also makes use of the "spinal Galant reflex" – as you stroke your fingers down your baby's back, along her spine, you may find her back automatically curves and she lifts her head in response. This reflex is present at birth, but usually starts to disappear from about three months.

Sensory integration

When you stroke your baby's back the tactile sensation encourages her to lift her head. This stimulates her proprioceptive system, which provides feedback from her muscles, joints and tendons, familiarizing her with the sensations involved in the movement. It improves head control and provides your baby with a new and stimulating view of the world.

What you will need
A towel
Your baby's favourite toy

Skills developed
Head and neck control

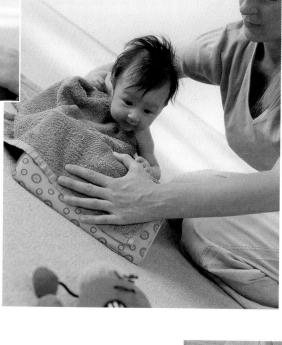

1 Lay your baby on her stomach and place her favourite toy in front of her, at a distance where she can lift her head and focus on it. To give her a bit more help, put a rolled-up towel or a foam wedge under her chest. This will shift her weight back, strengthening the muscles around her upper spine.

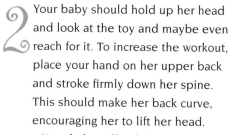

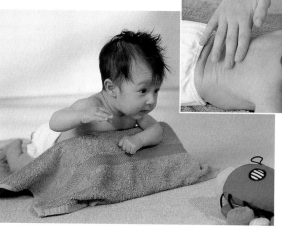

2 Your baby should hold up her head and look at the toy and maybe even reach for it. To increase the workout, place your hand on her upper back and stroke firmly down her spine. This should make her back curve, encouraging her to lift her head.

Your baby will only be able to stay on her stomach for a short period. Rather than prolonging this activity, repeat a few times each day.

Feathers and dusters

To really heighten your baby's sense of her body you could try this sensory stimulation game with her. First, gather together all the soft objects you can find around your home – a scarf, a velvet glove, a new feather duster, a plush toy. Next, undress your baby and lay her on her back. Put your face close to her and talk to her softly. Use the soft objects to gently stroke her all over her face and body. Watch how she reacts as you stroke her with different objects and on different areas of her body.

lifting and walking

With a little help, even a very tiny infant can hold his head up while being moved from a lying down to an upright position. The secret? Before lifting your baby, first roll him from his back to his side. This will keep his head in a straight line with his body and prevent it from flopping back and forth. Such a simple movement will boost your baby's development tremendously and give his neck muscles an excellent workout.

Once your baby is upright, you can hold him with his feet touching the floor and let him take some of his weight on his legs. This will help him build an awareness of his lower body. Young babies usually respond to being held in a standing position with a reflexive "walking" action. Try introducing this activity at a baby group meeting. Have each adult "walk" his or her child towards another baby and see the concentration on all the faces turn to smiles.

Sensory integration

This type of head control is an adaptive response requiring input from the eyes and the muscles in the neck, and incorporating your infant's inner ear balance. At this age, supported walking is still an instinctive reaction to body sensations, but it may be useful for honing the muscle patterns and neural pathways necessary for later, independent walking.

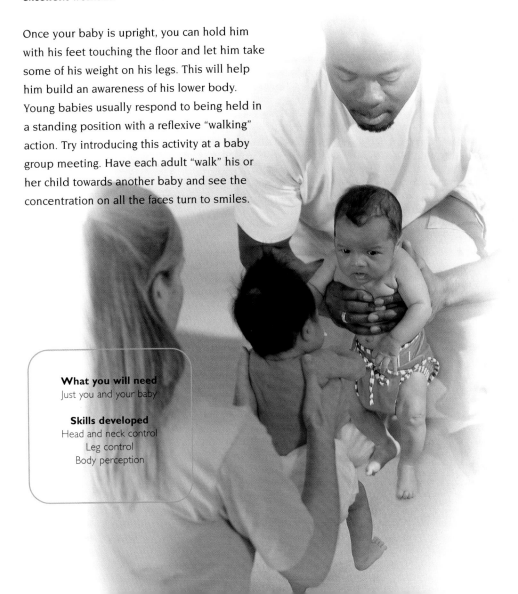

What you will need
Just you and your baby

Skills developed
Head and neck control
Leg control
Body perception

1 Take hold of your baby around his chest and roll him onto his side. This will prevent his head from flopping too far forward or back as you lift him, helping him hold up his head. Even quite young babies will soon learn to support their heads when lifted in this way.

2 Lean your baby forward with his feet touching the floor. One foot should lift automatically and step forward, followed by the other. Your baby is walking – with your help. Keep a firm grip – baby doesn't have the balance to support himself – and follow his lead. He will enjoy his changing perspective. This reflex is strongest around three weeks and disappears at around two to three months.

WATCH OUT!

At six weeks of age, the cervical area and neck muscles are still weak. Larger babies in particular may need extra time to learn how to control their heavier heads. Try turning your baby onto her stomach – if she is unable to raise her head off the surface, you should give a little more time for her neck muscles to develop. Don't hold off for too long, though – the more chance she has to support her own head, the more opportunity her muscles will have to develop. Always remember to roll her onto her side before lifting, so that her head doesn't flop.

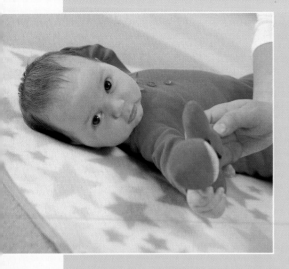

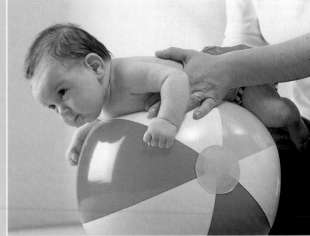

from two to three months

When a two- to three-month-old baby spots a shiny or colourful object nearby, she expresses her excitement with her entire body. If one of her hands happens to touch the object of desire, she will reflexively grasp it. A chance touch to her feet will cause her to kick her legs wildly.

At this stage, most babies can briefly fixate in midline – that is, focus their gazes directly in front of them as opposed to the newborn tendency to look off to the side. Your baby can now track from the side to midline, from midline to the side, and is also beginning to track across the midline. This is a major milestone: the development of effective head control and visual awareness is a significant step towards developing skills that will enable your baby to fully interact with her environment.

Opportunities to explore the sense of touch increase your baby's visual as well as tactile senses. The activities in this chapter provide a variety of age-appropriate stimulation, but don't feel you have to stop at these suggestions. You could collect various brightly coloured and "touchy-feely" objects from your living space and touch them to your child's hands or feet. Notice the reaction – soon you will see that your baby does not wait to have the object brought to her, but will deliberately guide her hands to her goal and grasp for it.

For successful playtime, be sure to choose a time when your baby is fed and well rested. Pay attention to your baby's cues and limit the time accordingly. You three-month-old infant signals her willingness to engage in play by both gazing at you and smiling, and her desire to end a bout of play by gazing away, frowning or crying. Your baby is giving you real feedback for the first time, so be sure to notice!

$grasp$ the rattle

A three-month-old baby can track objects both horizontally and vertically within a short visual range. Her vision is not yet fully mature – she won't be able to follow objects smoothly across the full range of vision until she is about four months old – but she is learning all the time.

Your baby also should begin to open her hands when extending her arms. This is because at around this stage, the grasp reflex, which is strongest in the first two months, begins to be replaced by a voluntary grasp. *Grasp the rattle* helps develop voluntary swiping and reaching motions and improves visual tracking.

Sensory integration

This grasping activity may seem simple, but it requires your baby's brain to organize a set of muscles she has never used before – quite a task for your little one. Your infant's sense of touch sends messages to her brain to help her to hold onto things – the development of a voluntary grasp is an "adaptive response" to this sensation. Another skill required in this activity is hand-eye coordination – this is the process by which the eye feeds information to the brain, the brain passes this information to the muscles and the muscles respond. Your baby needs a lot of practice to master both of these skills.

What you will need
A favourite teething ring
or rattle

Skills developed
Visual tracking
Hand-eye coordination
Object handling

1 Place your baby gently on her back. First make eye contact by putting your face close to your baby's and talking softly and then shake the rattle lightly to attract her attention.

2 Offer your baby the rattle at chest level (putting it in front of her face can be intimidating). Give her the option of choosing which hand to use rather than encouraging any hemisphere dominance. If your baby does not seem to notice the rattle, lightly touch it to her chest to help her get a visual fix on it.

3 Give her time to reach with her chosen hand to catch the rattle. She may hold it for a few seconds before dropping it. Once it is out of her hand she will instantly forget about it – what baby cannot see does not exist – so you should pick it up and offer it to her again.

How does your baby grow?

At this age, your baby will not be able to release her grip intentionally. When her wrist is straight, she is likely to hold on to an object; when her wrist is flexed, her fingers extend and she will drop an object without noticing – this is effect is called tenodesis. It won't be until your baby reaches around nine or 10 months of age that she will really start to get the hang of letting things go.

roll over

Giving your baby the opportunity for some "tummy time" will increase his head control and give him a chance to view his environment from a different angle. Although babies should be put to sleep on their backs, parents often extend this practice to their waking hours. The result is babies who later resist being placed on their stomachs, spend too much time staring at the ceiling, and do not have the neck muscles necessary for easy crawling.

When you roll baby onto his stomach and encourage him to lift his head, his efforts are rewarded by a view of more interesting and stimulating surroundings than when lying on his back staring at the ceiling. With better head control, his visual attention in the face-down position improves. Eventually he will be able to track horizontally up to 180 degrees.

Sensory integration

As your baby lifts his head or rolls over, fluid in his inner ear keeps his brain informed about the balance and motion of his head. He also receives feedback from his muscles and visually from his changing view of the world. The combination of these different senses – vestibular, proprioceptive and visual – helps him develop good postural reactions, body awareness and visual tracking.

What you will need
Just you and your baby

Skills developed
Visual tracking
Body awareness

1. Lay your baby gently on his back and hold a finger within range of his reach. Move your finger over to one side and watch him follow it with his eyes, hands and body.

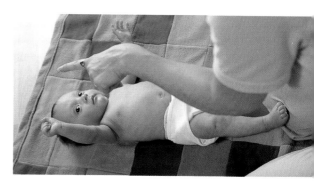

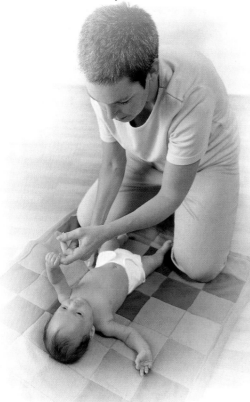

2. He should try to reach for and grasp your finger. This will cause his shoulder to move in the same direction and he may then shift onto his tummy. If not, help him by placing a finger behind his knee and pushing gently to help him roll over.

Sausage roll

For a slightly more playful variation, use a towel to roll your baby back and forth. Place the towel flat on your bed or another soft surface and lay baby on her back towards one end. Slowly lift the edge of the towel so she rolls onto her side and then her tummy – she may initially try to resist by pushing her arm against the towel, but she should soon get the idea. Give her a little time to re-orient herself, then roll her slowly onto her back again.

3. Let him do as much as possible without your help. If an arm is stuck under his stomach, lift his body slightly where the arm is wedged and he should be able to bring it forward by himself. If he still has difficulties, gently stroke his arm – the additional stimulation will remind his brain to respond. Be sure to practice this activity on both sides, particularly if you notice that your baby is stronger on one side than the other.

pushing and reaching

At two to three months your baby starts to enjoy kicking. His leg movements will become stronger and he will start to make rhythmic, circular motions in the air. By around three months, you may notice that his hip and knee joints are becoming more flexible and he is better able to direct his body. The early standing and walking reflexes are starting to disappear and your baby's understanding of how his body moves is improving every day.

This activity is designed to increase the strength in your baby's legs. Unlike more passive exercises – manipulating your baby's legs in a cycling motion, for example – this activity encourages the active participation of your baby, who needs to push against your hands to propel himself forward.

Sensory integration

The aim of this activity is to encourage your baby to head for a toy just out of reach. It depends on his ability to move himself and shift his weight to operate his arm away from his body. These early postural reactions help him lift up his head and, later, roll over and get onto his hands and knees.

> **What you will need**
> A selection of toys
>
> **Skills developed**
> Head and neck control
> Body perception
> Leg strength and control

1 Place your baby gently on his tummy. If he is uncomfortable in this position, put a rolled-up towel under his chest to support his upper body. Place a toy a little distance in front of him, just out of his reach.

2 Bend his legs slightly and place the bottom of his feet in your palms. To reach for the toy, he will push against your hands – keep exerting pressure against his bent legs to enable him to move towards his goal. By the end of the third month his strength should increase enough for him to stretch out his arms on his own.

3 Once he has reached the toy, let him claim his reward. Don't push the toy further in front of him or he will become disheartened. Tell him how well he has done and let him play with his toy.

WATCH OUT!

This activity is not suitable right after feeding – the excitement and the pressure on your baby's tummy may lead to a messy floor! Always remember to recognize your baby's efforts and show your pleasure with him.

beach ball fun

Balls are great fun for children of all ages so your baby should really enjoy this activity – and it also benefits her whole body. This exercise stimulates head lifting and the forward movement of your baby's arms. Her leg muscles will be strengthened by the need to support her body and her toes will get an great workout from all that kicking. Let your baby go barefoot – her toes will get a better sense of the ground and give her a real feel for the activity.

Sensory integration

As your baby rolls back and forth, the movement stimulates her vestibular and proprioceptive systems, providing her brain with feedback from the inner ear and from her muscles and joints. As she learns to organize and react to these sensations, your baby will start to hold her head up against gravity and may experiment by pushing her feet against the ground.

> **What you will need**
> Beach ball around 20–30 cm (10–12 in) in diameter – bigger if you have a good-sized baby
>
> **Skills developed**
> Head, neck and shoulder control
> Leg control

Older babies

You can repeat this activity with an older baby, this time placing a rattle or toy on the floor in front of the ball and encouraging her to reach for it. Or try placing a mirror on the floor so your baby can see her reflection when you bring her forward.

1 Place your baby face down with her upper body on the ball, letting her feet touch the ground – if they do not touch the ground, the ball is too big. Your baby should lift up her head and look around.

2 Supporting your baby from behind, rock her slowly back and forth. It is easier and more comfortable for both of you if you hold your baby with open hands, so that your thumbs are on her back and your fingers on the ball. Be sure to hold on to your baby as well as the ball!

3 Give your baby the chance to touch the ground and kick her feet. With the ball supporting most of her body weight she should be able to push herself up using her toes. Repeat this activity as often as she likes – as she gets the hang of the exercise she should start to stretch, wiggle and point her toes on the way up, then uncurl them again ready for landing.

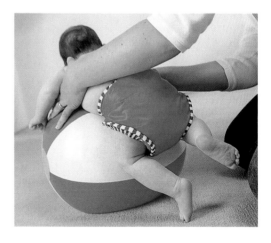

ticking clock

Young babies greatly enjoy the feeling of motion, although at this age they still largely rely on their parents to provide these sensations. The simple side-to-side motion in this activity will not only amuse and entertain your baby but will also help to strengthen the muscles in his neck, shoulders and upper torso.

Bear in mind that there's a fine line between the right amount of stimulation and too much. You may be tempted to play more rough-house or even throw him in the air, but this is not the right time to do so; at this age his neck muscles are not well enough developed.

Sensory integration
Sensations of gravity and movement are extremely pleasing to babies. Lifting, rocking and other types of gentle vestibular and proprioceptive stimulation will often calm a fussy or upset baby. As your child

learns to make sense of these sensations, his head control and general body awareness will improve. Motor control tends to progress from the head downwards and from the centre of the body outwards, and your baby needs to develop good head, shoulder and torso control before he can learn to manipulate his fingers and his toes.

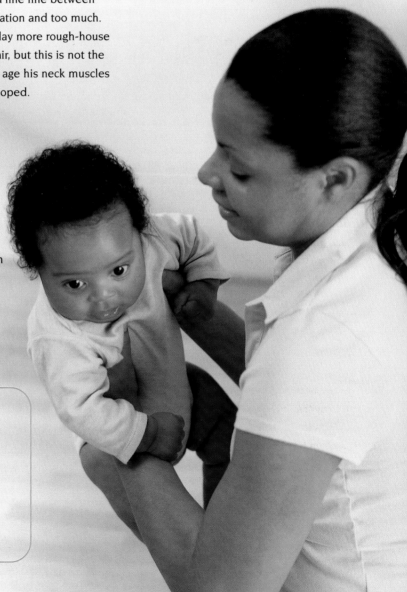

What you will need
Just you and your baby

Skills developed
Head and neck control
Upper and lower body
alignment

1 Place your baby on his back and take hold of him with your open fingers under his armpits and thumbs around his chest. This will enable you to grasp him without too much pressure on his chest so he can breathe easily.

2 Lift your baby straight up in front of you to get his attention. As always, be sure to turn him slightly to the side before lifting, so that he can hold his head as an extension of his trunk.

3 Lean your baby slowly to the right and back to the centre, then to the left and back to the centre – like the pendulum of a clock. As you do so, you might like to make tick-tock sounds. Repeat on both sides five or six times. However, if you have small hands and a large baby, you may prefer fewer repetitions.

WATCH OUT!

At two months you should not tilt your baby's body more than about 45 degrees. Any further than this and he may have problems holding his head upright. The older he is and the stronger his neck muscles become, the further you can tilt him – but never tilt him so far to the side that he cannot hold his head in line with his spine.

glove mobile

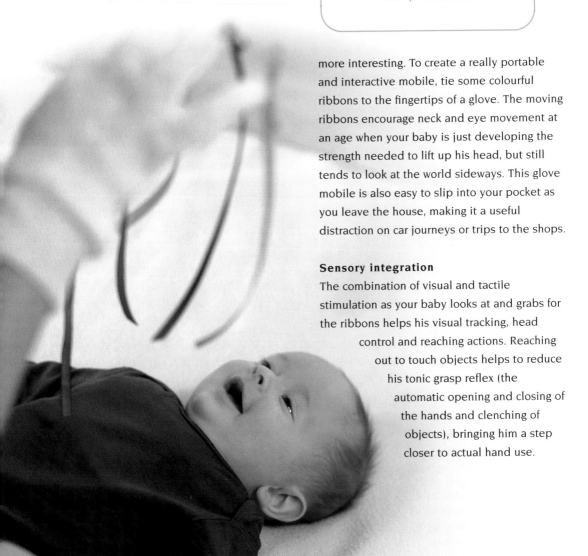

Colourful moving objects are very intriguing to babies in this age group. Rather than simply fixing a shop-bought mobile to the ceiling or to your baby's cot, a portable one that can be moved closer to his field of vision and which he can reach out and play with, will prove much

What you will need
A cotton glove
Lengths of ribbon in different colours

Skills developed
Head and neck control
Visual tracking
Hand-eye coordination

more interesting. To create a really portable and interactive mobile, tie some colourful ribbons to the fingertips of a glove. The moving ribbons encourage neck and eye movement at an age when your baby is just developing the strength needed to lift up his head, but still tends to look at the world sideways. This glove mobile is also easy to slip into your pocket as you leave the house, making it a useful distraction on car journeys or trips to the shops.

Sensory integration
The combination of visual and tactile stimulation as your baby looks at and grabs for the ribbons helps his visual tracking, head control and reaching actions. Reaching out to touch objects helps to reduce his tonic grasp reflex (the automatic opening and closing of the hands and clenching of objects), bringing him a step closer to actual hand use.

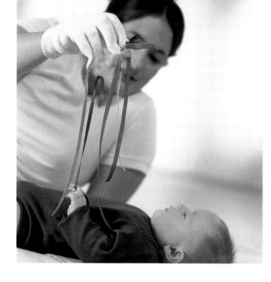

1 Get your baby's attention by waving the ribbons at chest level or touch his chest with them. Do not place the ribbons too close to his face or you may upset him.

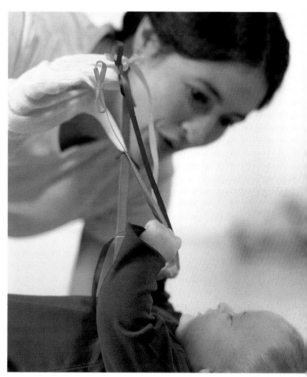

2 Move the glove from the centre point to baby's right, then back to centre and to his left. Move it up above his head, then down to below eye level. This will encourage visual tracking and head control.

3 Stop the glove at chest level and let your baby reach for and grab the dangling ribbons. The older baby gets, the quicker he will be able to grab at it.

How does your baby grow?

Observe how your infant can now freely turn her head to each side and can briefly hold it steady at the midline. The ability to visually track an object in this way helps your baby to develop a full range of neck motion. You may notice that she becomes more responsive and her attention span increases as her ability to keep an object or person in her line of vision improves.

who's in the mirror?

For a two-month-old baby, out of sight is out of mind. But throughout her first year, your baby gradually comes to understand that people and things continue to exist even though she can't see them. This concept, known as "object permanence" is a major developmental milestone.

If you haven't tried the exercise on pages 20–21, try to introduce your baby to mirrors by around two months. She will look into the mirror and see her own face first and then see you. She may be surprised that you are both holding her and looking at her from the mirror – a sign that the notion of object permanence has begun to develop. Playing this type of hiding game will make your baby more accustomed to having a face disappear and reappear, which will help her learn that the world, despite constantly changing, does remain consistent and reliable.

> **What you will need**
> Medium-sized, non-breakable mirror
>
> **Skills developed**
> Visual tracking
> Awareness of object permanence

Sensory integration

A mirror is a very effective way to stimulate your newborn's visual and cognitive development because it provides an ever-changing view of the world. Your baby uses these visual cues as she learns to differentiate between reflected images and the real world.

1 Place your baby gently on her back. Hold the mirror around 25 cm (10 in) in front of her face so that she can see herself reflected. Let her touch the mirror if she wants to – this extra tactile information helps her distinguish between reflections and reality. Lift the mirror a few inches upwards so that your baby's eyes follow.

2 Change the angle of the mirror so that you can see your baby's reflection in the mirror. This means she can see yours. Move in and out of the mirror's reflection, saying "peek-a-boo" each time you reappear. Observe your baby's reaction. Blinking is a sign of your baby's curiosity and shows that she is making critical use of visual information – she closes and then opens her eyes to check whether the image changes.

Older babies

You could play a game similar to hide-and-seek using scarves of varying colours and sizes – some opaque, some translucent, some so small they only cover your face and some large enough to hide you both. This game helps introduce your baby to the idea that people and things can keep their identity even though certain aspects can change. Try hiding your face and then pulling away the scarf to reveal yourself again. You could try putting the scarf (briefly) over your baby's face. She may try to remove it from her face herself, or you can pull it slowly away for her.

kick the ball

At around three months of age, most babies enjoy rhythmically kicking their legs. The kicking action helps develop the muscles and motor skills your baby will need later, when he learns to walk. Using balls to provide a light weight for your baby to kick against makes him much more conscious of his legs and hips; with some babies, simply touching the ball to their feet will stimulate the legs to lift up and kick. Your baby will really enjoy this activity – the

What you will need
String, yarn or ribbon
2–3 light balls in various sizes

Skills developed
Kicking action
Body perception

presence of something to move against makes the basic kicking activity much more satisfying, while the movement of the ball helps him learn about cause and effect.

Sensory integration

Contact with the balls helps to stimulate your baby's proprioceptive system – the sensation of the balls on the soles of his feet encourages his muscles to stretch and contract and his joints to bend. Combined with the visual treat of seeing the balls bounce as he kicks them, this helps his healthy physical development.

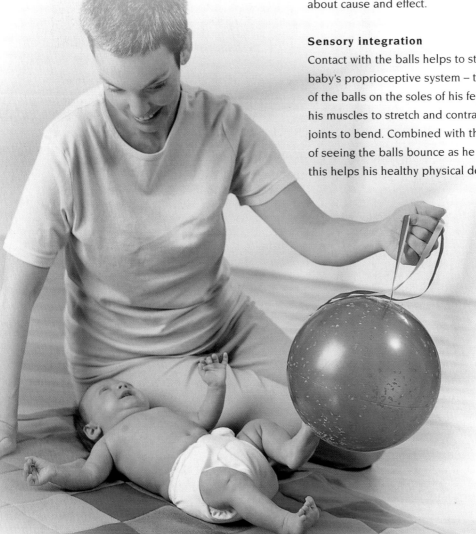

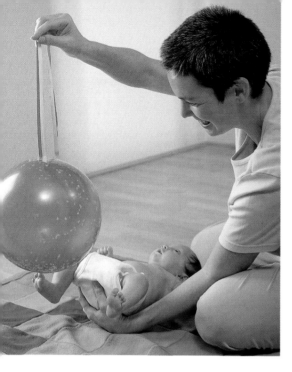

1 Attach a length of ribbon, string, or yarn to the surface of a light ball. Tie the ribbon to the nozzle, if the ball has one, or stick it on with strong tape. Place your baby gently on his back, put your hand under his bottom to elevate his legs, and use your free hand to dangle the ball in front of his feet.

2 Rest the ball against your baby's feet to encourage him to kick out. Initially, he may only kick the ball by accident, but as he sees and feels it move he will come to realize that he can reproduce the same effect on purpose. In this way he learns that he is able to influence the world around him.

3 Once your baby gets the hang of the exercise, repeat it using other balls in various sizes. Changing the size of the balls will teach your baby to adjust his kick.

How does your baby grow?

At two months your baby may seem to move his legs without purpose, kicking objects by accident rather than design – but he'll soon become more familiar with the sensations. By three months he should start showing much more coordination. By four months your baby may be able to touch and grab the ball between his feet and by five months may even demonstrate enough hand-foot coordination to transfer it all the way from his feet to his hands.

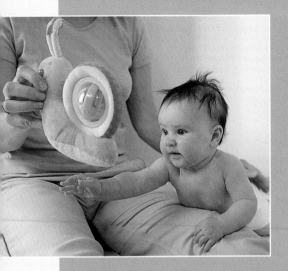

3

from four to five months

Your baby now has some control over her movements. There is a time of disorganization as motor learning begins, but soon even the most passive infant successfully experiments with movement – both of individual parts and of the entire body.

From the fourth or fifth month and throughout the first year, motor activity accelerates as your infant learns to move and control her body in space. Displaying tremendous energy, she practices gross motor patterns repeatedly, and often becomes frustrated if unable to move from one position to another. Although some babies are less active in total body movements, they repeat other motor patterns such as sucking, reaching and grasping toys, or playing with their fingers and feet.

Your baby will learn to reach out with certainty towards an object and manipulate it. This develops coordination of sight, touch and movement and is

the basis for the perception of depth, the physical properties of objects and many other characteristics such as shape, size, surface or weight. Suspend a toy above your baby and notice the way her hand approaches the object, how she learns to control her movements, her understanding of object shape, position and distance. Once she wraps her hands around something, she'll study it using all her senses.

At this age, baby loves to put everything she can find into her mouth. The mouth is a much more important sensory organ for the baby than it is for the older child – an older child who has started talking loses interest in this type of investigation. When your baby puts something in her mouth, she starts constructing a mental model of the object in her brain and learning more about her environment. This is very important, but that doesn't mean that she has to put everything into her mouth. Be certain that the objects within her reach are non-toxic and large enough to avoid a choking hazard.

fascinating feet

As your four-month-old baby's stomach and thigh muscles strengthen, she should be able to lift her legs and touch her knees with her hands. By the fifth or sixth month of life she should be able to grasp her feet and stick them into her mouth, making use of her increasing control over her upper and lower extremities.

Observe your infant's developing hand-to-foot play and eye-hand coordination – you could make a pair of rattle socks to really draw her attention. As she targets her feet she may at first under-reach, but she soon learns to adjust her aim and grasp hold. Your baby's ability to

What you will need
Bells, sequins and other small shiny objects
A pair of baby socks

Skills developed
Coordination of both sides of the body
Hip control
Hand-eye coordination

sustain this mid-position for hand-to-foot play indicates she is learning to balance and control her hip flexor and extensor muscles. The interplay between these muscles will be necessary, later, for sitting and stability.

Sensory integration
This activity encourages your baby to continue developing body awareness through self-exploration and tactile and auditory stimulation. It encourages the coordination of the part of the brain she uses when seeing with the part of the brain she uses when touching.

1 Sew some attention-grabbing baubles such as bells, beads, sequins or buttons onto a pair of baby socks. Lay your baby face up and place the socks on her feet. If necessary, lift her bottom and move her feet to get her attention.

2 Observe how your baby plays with and reaches for her feet. By six months your baby should be playing with two hands on one foot – this indicates development of good midline awareness and the ability to cross midline. If your baby manages to pull any of the objects off the socks, take them away before she tries to put them into her mouth.

Bouncing Balloons

Take some good-quality balloons. Inside each one place an object or substance that will make noise when the balloon is shaken. Bells, sand, water, pasta – use your imagination. Blow the balloons up and tie a length of ribbon to each one.

Lay your baby on her back and hold each balloon, one by one, over her chest. The objects in the balloons will keep them from floating too high in the air, and provide a satisfying weight for her to grab, kick or punch. If baby gets tired of lying down, put her on her tummy to encourage neck control. You could even sit her up, provided you support her under her arms with your hands – her lower back is not yet strong enough to support her weight.

reach for it

At this age, improved visual, tactile and motor skills allow your baby to make more consistent contact with toys. She enjoys bringing them to her mouth to investigate more closely, and is better able to explore and examine objects by touch. Your baby doesn't just enjoy looking at mobiles, she also wants to reach out and touch them.

To create a really stimulating mobile for baby to play with you should make your own. You could use a small laundry rack and clip objects onto it – this lets you easily swap objects around and change the selection. Babies are especially attracted to faces, so draw or cut out faces of babies or, better still, use photographs of family members or relatives. Be sure to cover these in contact paper or some sort of plastic lamination so that baby won't be affected by paper dyes or photo chemicals.

Sensory integration

This projects helps your child to develop an awareness of where her hands are in space. She needs her sense of touch, the sensations from her muscles and joints (proprioception), as well as her vision if she is to learn to use her hands accurately.

What you will need
Small laundry rack or materials to make a mobile
Colourful objects to hang on the mobile

Skills developed
Hand-eye coordination
Object handling

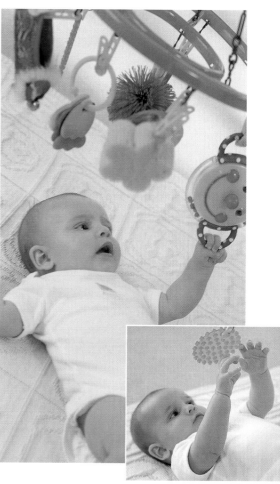

1 Lay your baby gently on her back and hang the homemade mobile over her head. At first she may be frightened of it, so put it a little distance away to give her a chance to get used to it – her curiosity should soon get the better of any timidity. Smile and talk to her.

2 Move the mobile to within reaching distance of your baby. Blow gently on the mobile to make it move or wave some of the dangling items to attract your baby's attention. She should try to reach out and grasp the different objects dangling above her.

3 Observe which objects your baby seems to prefer. What does she like to look at or grab? Change the objects on your handmade mobile regularly to keep your baby both interested and stimulated.

WATCH OUT!

Babies find homemade toys, such as this mobile, every bit as fascinating as more expensive shop-bought toys, but you do need to take care to make them safe. If your baby is quick and fairly strong, she will pull objects off the mobile and put them in her mouth, so choose toys that cannot break and do not present a choking hazard.

see it and go for it

Around the fourth or fifth month, your baby learns to reach out with certainty towards an object and will try to manipulate it. This obviously requires a measure of hand control, but the ability to locate and reach for an object also involves considerable body control and coordination.

This type of reaching activity helps with focusing, strengthens your baby's neck muscles and helps develop upper body control. In trying to grab the toy, your baby may even start to push away using her other arm or push off with her legs if she has something behind her. This weight-shifting response is the basis of all normal reciprocal locomotion, including crawling, creeping, climbing and walking.

Sensory integration

The adaptive response of reaching helps the brain to develop and organize itself. It requires the coordination of sight, touch and depth perception, as well as the realization that objects have shape, size, surface or weight. Nobody can make an adaptive response for a child – it is something that she must do for herself.

What you will need
Your baby's favourite toy

Skills developed
Visual tracking
Upper body control from
head to hips
Reaching and pushing actions

1 Sit on the ground with your legs extended. Lay your baby face down with her chest resting on one leg, so that her shoulders and arms can move freely. Pick her favourite colourful toy and let her watch it moving in the air. Move the toy slowly to the right, to the left, up, down and in a circular and diagonal motion. The greater your child's field of vision the greater her curiosity and the more enthusiastically she'll reach for it.

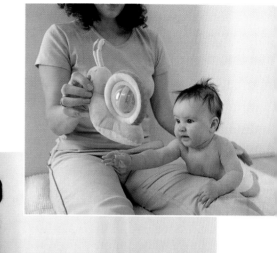

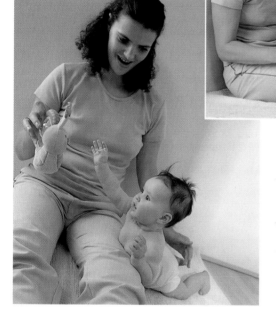

Doing the airplane

It is exciting to watch infants doing "the airplane" – balancing on their tummies with hands and legs up in the air as if they were flying. This also provides a great photo opportunity, as babies usually display either a look of determination or of glee. Lay your baby on your lap to make her feel like she is moving through the air. To really elicit a giggle from your little one, try doing the airplane on the floor next to her!

2 Put the toy a little out of your child's reach to encourage her to stretch further. Place one hand behind her legs to give her something to push against. If your baby is desperate to get the toy, do give it to her – this activity is supposed to be fun! After a little pause, let her try again.

standing tall

Around the fourth month of life, the strength of your baby's grasp starts to increase enough for her to be able to keep hold of your fingers as you pull her up into a sitting or standing position. By five months, she may even be able to bend her elbows to chest level to pull herself up. If your baby is able to bend her arms slightly without lifting her shoulders it is a sign that she is strong enough to carry on pulling until she is standing. Your five-month old should also be able to take almost all of her weight on her legs. Notice how your own body moves when progressing from sitting to standing up – this can be helpful in guiding your little one.

This activity is not meant to teach your baby to sit or stand – this should come naturally and depends on your baby's own rate of development. Rather, this exercise is intended to encourage visual fixing to reinforce head stability, to improve her ability to grab, and to develop good abdominal, hip and knee control. It will also strengthen her leg muscles and help increase her balance.

Sensory integration
As your child learns to assimilate the information coming in from her different senses, her muscles are able to respond to changes in her body position by contracting to keep her body upright and control her movements.

What you will need
Just you and your baby

Skills developed
Control and balance of the whole body

1 Gently position your baby on her back and offer her your forefingers to grab. Put your thumbs over her hands to give a better grip in case she releases her hold involuntarily. You may have to arrange her legs so they are not crossed.

2 When your baby has a good hold, turn her upper body slightly to one side, so her head stays in line with her trunk, and bring your hands towards your chest. Try to get her to pull herself up if possible. She will lift her head, bend her elbows, and come to a sitting position.

3 When bringing your baby into a standing position, pull her slowly forward. When her knees are in line with her feet, she should stand up by herself without you needing to pull. Talk to your baby so her eyes stay focused on your face, with her head erect. Give her a big smile once she is standing.

Older babies

 Try the same exercise using a chopstick or a long wooden spoon. This requires your baby to adjust his grasp and his body without your help, improving his confidence. Keep one hand behind your baby's back in case he releases his grasp on the stick and falls back.

4 Gently push your baby's hands back to help her sit down again, controlling her with her bending arms. From this position, guide her back down until she is lying on her back once again.

lift off

At five months of age your baby is entering an active phase. She adores to be pulled up and, with a little help, she makes a great jumper. Her back and neck muscles are now strong enough to keep her body upright; her legs bend and extend on landing and lift off; and her stomach muscles tense to support the weight on her hips and legs. Indeed, you may well find that your baby can't seem to get enough of this type of activity – the up and down motion increases her visual range and provides a stimulating and invigorating workout. You should certainly stop if she shows any signs of tiredness – but you are more likely to find that it's your arms that are the first to grow weary.

Sensory integration

Your infant should now be able to integrate her sense of gravity with her sense of movement. The kinesthetic stimulation provided by the up and down movement of this exercise stimulates your child's sense of spatial orientation and balance

(the vestibular system) – all of which helps to enhance her motor development. You only need to take a look at your baby's face to see how exciting this type of vestibular stimulation can be.

What you will need
Just you and your baby

Skills developed
Leg control Body perception
Spatial orientation

1 Take hold of your baby just under the arms and lift her to a standing position – remembering to turn her slightly to one side as you lift so she is able to support her head. Your baby's feet should touch the ground gently, with her feet flat.

Squelchy sacks

Fill some heavy-duty Ziploc freezer bags with different volumes of water. Add a few drops of food colouring to each bag as well as a few objects such as some pieces of raw vegetable. Use cool water for some, warm water for others. Baby will feel the weight of the bag in one hand and perhaps transfer it to the other. Put the bag on different parts of her body to introduce her to different sensations.

2 Slowly lower your baby towards the ground so her knees bend. Then help her push upwards off the ground until her legs are fully extended. Continue to lift her up through the air in front of you.

3 Lift your baby up high above you. She should laugh happily at the feeling of moving through the air. Give her a smile and lots of encouragement. Then bring her back to the standing position and repeat the exercise as often as she likes.

4

from six to seven months

Your little baby is now quite active. He rolls over. He moves his body from side to side. He may even be crawling. He is becoming increasingly independent. Are you ready for it? Expect spilled plants and toppled chairs – all in the name of research, of course.

At this stage, the instinctive need to be upright is strong, and baby's first attempts to get up on his hands and knees can frustrate him. The following activities help gain the muscle strength and coordination to move on all fours. Hand or foot play is also important from a tactile and visual perspective.

Your baby is also developing a fairly accurate reach and improving his fine motor skills – the use of his fingers and hands in small, coordinated movements. Once he has learned to grab a toy, he may start to practice moving it from one hand to the other. The ability to reach for and manipulate objects is another skill highlighted in this chapter.

Beware of comparing your child's development to that of other children the same age or to charts or checklists in textbooks. Your child is unique. He will reach each milestone only when he is physically, mentally, cognitively and socially ready for it. The pace of development, particularly at seven months, can be noticeably different from baby to baby. You have to respect your baby's individual development, so don't rush him!

Whether your baby crawls at six months or at ten months matters little in the grand scheme of his life. These activities are not designed to make him a champion gymnast or track star, or even to give him a "leg-up" on his peers. They are meant to give you an appreciation for the wonder of your child's development, to give you an excuse and a structure for playing together, and to help you set aside some quality time together.

fun with feathers

Babies are fascinated by feathers – the softer and more colourful the better. Use one to stroke your baby from top to toe so that she gets a sense of where her body starts and finishes. Place the feather between her toes so that she stretches both hands out to reach for it. This teaches her to control her hand movements by sight, which develops her visual-motor coordination and improves control over her lower limb movements as well.

Sensory integration
This exercise works primarily on your baby's tactile system. Her sense of touch sends messages to her brain that help her to orient her sight to the source of the stimulation. She then integrates the touch sensation from the muscles and joints of her arms, hands, legs and feet to bring them together and reach for the feather with one or both hands. By bringing one hand across the centre of her body to her opposite foot, she can gradually grasp the feather more efficiently, using a pincer grip. Crossing her midline is crucial to the balanced development of the right and left hemispheres of her brain.

What you will need
A brightly coloured feather, about 10–25 cm (4–10 in) long

Skills developed
Hand-eye coordination
Dissociation of upper and lower body
Hip flexibility

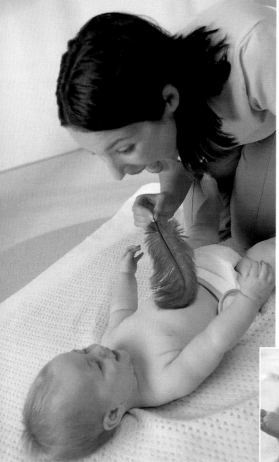

1 Lay your baby gently on her back and wave the feather in front of her to attract her attention. Use the feather to stroke her body from the crown of her head to the tips of her toes.

2 Now try to place the feather between two of her toes. If she doesn't seem to notice it there, lift her leg to show it to her. This provides visual stimulation and promotes hand–eye coordination as she tries to reach for the feather.

3 Once your baby has grabbed the feather, allow her to play with it for as long as she likes – but be alert in case she puts it into her mouth. Next, ask her for the feather. At first you will probably just pull it out of her grasp, but you can thank her as if she did hand it to you.

How does your baby grow?

Do this exercise regularly and you will be able see how your baby's reactions to stimulation change and develop over time:

Does she seem more tactile or visual at the moment?

Does she spread or curl her toes when you put the feather between them?

Does she try to spread her fingers to the size of the feather?

Does she transfer the feather from one hand to the other or put it straight into her mouth?

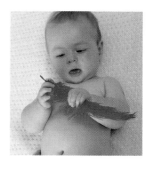

somersault

As your baby grows older, he needs to learn how to orient his body in space – this exercise will help get him used to the different sensations. He may initially feel disoriented when his head is in the air and when you roll him back to the ground, but after a few tries he will soon learn to adjust to whatever position he finds himself in. The more confident you are when lifting your baby onto your shoulder, the more at ease your baby will feel.

Once on your shoulder, your baby will enjoy looking around and will lift his head, which reinforces his upper body muscles. This type of vestibular stimulation provides a great way for him to explore his world from lots of different angles.

What you will need
Just you and your baby

Skills developed
Back muscle development
Hip flexibility
Spatial awareness

Sensory integration
Vestibular information is processed, together with information from your baby's proprioceptive system and from his vision, in the cerebral cortex. This information lets your baby know where he is in space and tells him how he should react to maintain his position and balance.

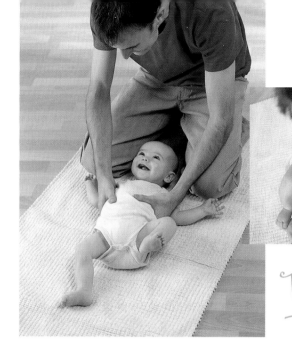

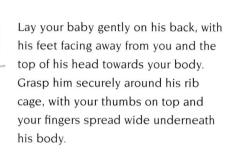

1 Lay your baby gently on his back, with his feet facing away from you and the top of his head towards your body. Grasp him securely around his rib cage, with your thumbs on top and your fingers spread wide underneath his body.

2 As always, turn your baby slightly to the side before lifting him. Then turn his body gently upside down and bring him up and onto one of your shoulders. If you turned him towards his left side he should end up on your left shoulder, and *vice versa*. He should stick out his arms and lift his head.

3 To return your baby to his initial position, put one hand on his bottom and the other hand behind his neck to support his head. Bend forward and roll him back down to the ground. His back and shoulders should reach the mat first. Talk to him and encourage him throughout the activity.

Superbaby

If you are feeling confident and your baby seems happy, try standing up and walking around with him on your shoulder airplane-style! And don't forget to smile and talk to your little one throughout.

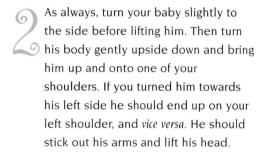

crawl for it

By six months most babies enjoy lying prone – they can push up onto their arms, shift their weight and reach out, and grasp toys of various sizes. If your baby is not enjoying the position, you may be giving her too much of an easy life by putting toys directly into her hands or so close that she doesn't have to work very hard to get them. Activities like this one will help stimulate and challenge her.

Your baby also has a strong desire to move forward, but she doesn't always have the ability – forward propulsion requires a combination of movements that more usually appear around the seventh month. But with a little bit of assistance – a guiding hand and a leg to push off against – your baby should be ready to make a start.

Sensory integration

Reaching helps your baby's brain develop and organize itself. As she reaches out and moves forward, she needs to coordinate her limbs and react to changes in information from different senses. Practicing these movements helps your baby understand the way her body functions.

What you will need
Your baby's favourite toy

Skills developed
Reaching and pushing actions
Rudimentary crawling action

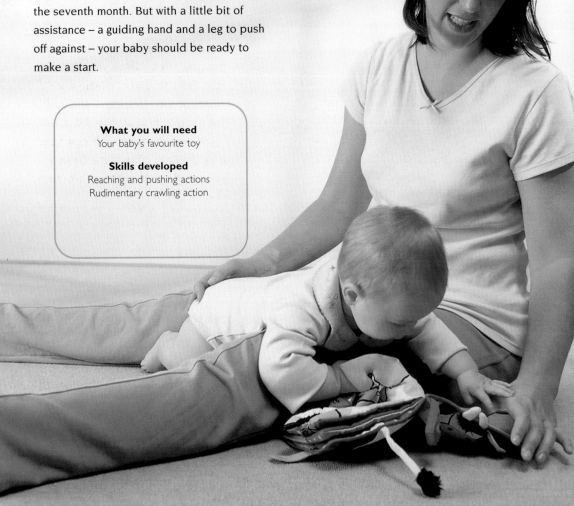

1 Sit on the floor with your legs straight out in front of you. Place your baby face down with her upper body resting on your left leg. She should have room to use her feet to push herself forward against your right leg.

2 Hold a toy just out of baby's reach to encourage her to "crawl" over your leg. She will start kicking and reaching for the toy, and in the process should start to move over your leg. Note how she uses her arms to push up off the floor. Set a hand on her bottom in case she rushes and loses her balance.

3 Kiss your baby when she arrives at her goal! Then turn her around to face the direction she came from and repeat the activity. If she gets the hang of this game easily, you could make it more challenging by rolling a little onto your side and encouraging her to climb up over your legs or hips.

How does your baby grow?

Your baby may experiment with all sorts of different methods of crawling before she settles on the conventional cross-crawling style:

She may drag herself across the floor on her tummy.

She may prefer to roll over and over across the floor to reach her goal.

She may try a commando-style crawl, resting on her elbows.

She may even use a reverse-crawling style, sitting on her bottom and pushing back with her arms.

sitting and reaching

At six to seven months, your baby is beginning to develop the trunk and hip control needed to stay upright when placed in a seated position. She may be able to sit independently on the floor, supporting her body with one arm on the ground. If you give her a little more support, she can lift both hands and may enjoy playing in this position.

What you will need
Your baby's favourite toy

Skills developed
Upper body control
Reaching action

In this activity you encourage your baby to reach for a toy placed just out of reach. You will probably still need to support her – as she turns her head to the side her weight will shift and she is likely to fall. However, the action of reaching out, even when followed by a fall, will help develop her perceptual and cognitive abilities. With each new movement she is learning more about gravity and about her own abilities.

Sensory integration
Information received from your baby's vestibular system contributes to the body perception and motor planning necessary to enable her to move from a sitting to a crawling position. It guides the movements of her entire body.

1 Sit your baby down, supporting her by the waist. Place a toy to the side of her, nearby at first. Your baby should turn her head towards the toy and then start to rotate her trunk and shoulders. She may place one hand on the floor to support her upper body, but keep a hand in front of her in case she falls. Let her play with the toy for a while before placing the toy on the other side of her body.

Going for a spin

Lay your baby face down. Set a favourite toy a little out of reach, but still in his visual field. Your baby will execute an amazing series of movements to reach the toy:

He will look at the toy and push his body up with his arms;
He will cross one arm over, free the arm that is under and extend it, then use his fingers to grab for the toy;
His upper body will pivot, his knees will bend to help his bottom lift and he will try to move foward;
He will repeat the same movement until he reaches the toy or becomes bored.

The more you play with him, the faster he will pivot and soon he will turn a full 360 degrees. This is an important skill for your baby that eventually will lead to him getting up on all fours and crawling.

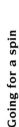

2 Push the toy a little out of reach. This will encourage your baby to lift her hips and get up on to her knees. She should switch to a crawling position or lie in a face-down position to better reach the toy. Let her play with the toy for a while before repeating this activity on the other side.

baby pull ups

On pages 52–3, we demonstrated how your baby can pull himself up to standing with the aid of your finger or a chopstick. At six to seven months, your little one should start learning how to pull himself up on any stationary object. When you first try this type of movement with him, he is still likely to need a helping hand or two. But eventually he should start using your body more like he would use a piece of furniture – as something strong and solid that he can hold on to while attempting to pull himself off the ground. Your baby will love the new perspective on the world that this upright position gives him.

Sensory integration

To balance himself, your baby is learning to place his legs in line with his hips and use the three supporting points of foot, foot and hand. He is learning how to control his body and stay stable while standing. This type of motor coordination and balance requires the integration of the vestibular, proprioceptive and tactile systems. As baby explores his environment from a standing position he can discover much more about height, distance and space.

What you will need
A stable object such as a chair
Your baby's favourite toy

Skills developed
Control and balance of the
whole body

1 Choose a stable, horizontal surface such as a chair or a coffee table – any surface that is higher than your baby's shoulders when sitting, but low enough to reach. Sit in front of this surface with one leg extended underneath it. Sit your little one astride that leg, but with his feet on the floor.

2 Put a toy on top of the surface, just out of baby's reach. He will try to get the toy by pushing down on the floor, leaning forward and standing up. He will probably get the toy and forget to hold on – so be ready to give him a bit of support!

3 Show your baby how to balance by holding on with one hand while grabbing the toy with the other. Put your hand over his and press gently so he can feel the secure weight of your hand. Repeat this activity two or three times so your baby understands how to do it. Eventually, he won't even need your leg to help him up!

How does your baby grow?

Your baby has to be able to pull himself up using furniture before he will be able to stand up using a flat surface such as a wall. From holding on to the wall, he will eventually let go – then it's only a toddler-sized step to that historic moment when he first starts to walk by himself.

learning to squat

Although your baby may now be standing up beautifully, she is probably still plopping back down ungracefully – or crying for you to help her because she can't work out how to sit down at all. The secret to sitting with elegance? Bending the knees – a whole new challenge!

This activity will help baby learn to bend her knees and, in time, she'll learn to sit daintily, too. When she reaches for the toy on the ground, she will place her feet apart for balance, shift her weight onto the leg nearest the toy, bend her knees and lower her buttocks – a very tricky sequence of movements for a little baby.

Sensory integration

By attempting and repeating various movements, your baby learns how to use her body in different situations. Depth, height, balance, control – all of these are important elements as your child learns to integrate and make use of the information she receives from her different senses.

> **What you will need**
> A stable object such as a chair
> Some favourite toys
>
> **Skills developed**
> Knees bending
> Control and balance of whole body

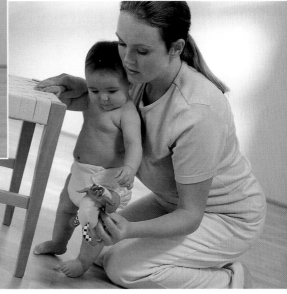

1 First, you need to be sure that your baby can stand against a stable object, such as a chair, without your support. Her two feet should be planted firmly on the ground about a shoulder-width apart. You should keep one hand on top of your baby's hand to help keep her upright.

2 Place a toy on the chair. Then, get your baby to follow the toy with her hand as you move it lower towards the ground. She will slowly begin to understand that by leaning forward and bending her knees a little she can still reach the toy.

Lift and crawl

At seven months most babies enjoy being on their tummies to explore, but not all babies are strong enough to push up on their arms. If your baby still has problems supporting his weight, he'll love a helping hand.

Fold a long towel lengthways and place your baby with his chest on the middle. Put a toy a good crawling distance in front of him. Lift the ends of the towel to bring your baby's body off the floor into a crawling position. Don't lift the towel too high – he has to carry some of his weight himself.

3 Get her to stand up again and place a few toys on the floor close to her feet. She may try to reach them without bending her knees. She may even fall onto her bottom, so be ready to stop her from collapsing. Eventually, she should work out that bending her knees is the solution.

ping-pong reflection

This is one of the most popular activities in the PEKiP programme. Babies are fascinated by the movement of the balls, the noise the balls make as they roll and bounce and the visual image of the balls – and of themselves – reflected in the mirror.

Watching your baby play this game, as she reaches out to grab hold of the balls, you may wonder whether your child is right- or left-handed. At this stage, it is still too early to tell – most babies seem to favour one hand for a while and then switch to the other. True right- or left-handedness won't be determined until she's two or three years old. In the meantime, give her the option of which hand to use rather than encouraging any hemisphere dominance.

Sensory integration

This stimulating game promotes good hand-eye coordination. You baby will soak up all the different sensory information – the sights and sounds, the feel of the balls as she grabs at them and puts them to her mouth – and in the process she'll learn some of the skills that she needs to make sense of her environment.

What you will need
A good sized, nonbreakable mirror
Ping-pong balls in various colours

Skills developed
Visual tracking
Hand-eye coordination
Head and neck control
Object handling

1 Place the mirror on the floor. Lay a rolled-up towel under your baby's chest to take the weight away from her shoulders, so that her arms can move freely. It will also make her more comfortable. Let your baby look at her reflection in the mirror.

2 Slowly roll one ball after another across the mirror, giving your baby time to work out what is going on. As she gets used to this, try bouncing, spinning and hitting the balls together. Or just place them in a line on top of the mirror.

3 Your baby will probably grab at the balls, and will make use of her fine motor skills to pick the balls up, bring them to her mouth, transfer them from one hand to another, or drop and bounce them.

5

from eight to nine months

Around the eighth, ninth or tenth month of life, your baby starts to master cross-crawling. He learns to alternate his arms and knees to move himself forward, with his right hand and left knee moving together, then his left hand and right knee. This coordinated movement of rear and front limbs is automatic, but you can promote your baby's body awareness by encouraging him to learn to negotiate the spaces under tables and chairs, to climb up and down steps and to explore all the other features of his environment.

Crawling is vitally important for the development of your baby's spine, back and neck muscles. You should therefore encourage crawling before sitting. Parents tend to focus too much on the latter, but babies will sit by themselves after they start crawling and there's no need to worry too much about coaching

them. By the eighth and ninth month, your baby should be sitting up straight and firmly enough to be able to turn round and lean forwards and backwards without losing his balance.

Your baby will now demonstrate a strong desire to move around and explore independently. His new mobility doesn't mean you will have more time for yourself – quite the opposite. His ability to reach a greater range of small objects – manipulating them, exploring them visually and bringing them to his mouth to investigate tactilely – will keep you running after him.

To baby, everything he can grab hold of is a toy and a curiosity, and you'll need to remove anything that is fragile or potentially harmful. You won't have to worry about keeping fit when you have a baby in the house!

on the go

In the last chapter your baby learned how to pull herself up using a piece of furniture. In this activity, she is learning to stand up using a flat surface, to cruise along using short, sideways steps, and finally to bend over to reach a toy on the floor. In this way your baby gains information about her entire body in relationship to space.

As you do this activity, talk your baby through what she is doing so that she learns to associate the movements she is making with basic concepts such as "up" and "down" or "here" and "there".

Sensory integration

Repetition of this type of activity, and the combination of gross and fine body movements, helps your baby improve her spatial awareness and gain the motor coordination that she needs to make smooth, accurate movements.

What you will need
Your baby's favourite toy

Skills developed
Spatial awareness
Control and balance of whole body

1 Help your baby stand upright and show her how to support herself by placing her hands flat against the back of a sofa or a wall. Keep your hands very close to your baby when she is standing, as she may get over-excited and lose her balance.

2 Place a toy a little way to the side, on a line just above baby's head and far enough away that she needs to take a few steps to reach it. Eventually, she will figure out how to transfer her weight and move one leg after the other, sideways, to reach for the object of her desire.

3 Place the toy on the floor beside your baby. As she tries to reach it she will learn to lean and lower her body, and then to crouch and pick up the toy. From there she may stand up straight again, sit or crawl away with her prize.

Jelly japes

You may have already been letting baby play with jelly while sitting in her highchair, but playing with it on the floor will be much more interesting. Put the jelly on a plastic mat, a baking tray or a mirror. If you decide to have your little one in the bath it will make things easier to clean up, but very slippery.

The idea is to stimulate as many of your baby's senses as possible. This game should use her sense of touch, vision, smell, and, of course, taste. Don't worry about your child eating the jelly – it is sticky, sweet and tasty, but it's also very tricky to grab!

double trouble

As sitting becomes more of a functional posture – meaning your baby is more willing to stay seated as she plays – it also becomes easier for her to manipulate objects using both hands. Prior to this, your baby would simply drop one toy as soon as she reached for the next. By now she is learning to handle more than one object at a time and may even be able to transfer a toy from one hand to the other.

As her manual control and dexterity improve, your baby should also learn to coordinate her thumb and index finger more effectively, using them together in a pincer grip. This type of delicate hand movement is closely connected to the development of play. It also affects your child's cognitive development – her ability to grasp small objects lets her manipulate and analyze their different characteristics, giving her a better understanding of the way the world works.

Sensory integration

Your baby's ability to handle more than one toy at a time, move an object from one hand to the other, and tap two toys together requires coordination between both sides of her body. She also needs fine control over her eye muscles to direct her gaze, good muscle control and awareness in her hands and arms and effective hand-eye coordination.

What you will need
Two small, similar toys such as ping-pong balls or wooden blocks

Skills developed
Object handling
Manual dexterity
Hand-eye coordination

1 Sit your baby opposite you, face to face. Take two ping-pong balls (or other small, nearly identical toys) and place one in each hand. Offer them to your baby by placing them on your palms. Encourage your baby to pick up the balls.

2 Observe how your baby attempts to do this. She may take only one ball and transfer it from one hand to the other. She may reach for both balls and drop one immediately, or she may hold on to both and bang them together. She will probably try putting them in her mouth to find out if they are hard or soft.

Lucky dip

Encourage your baby's curiosity by placing objects of varying textures – soft, rough, cold, hard – inside a basket or similar container. She will probably put some of the objects in her mouth, so keep this in mind when choosing.

Some objects will feel pleasurable on the tongue and hands, others may be strange – all part of the learning experience. Babies tend to empty the basket quickly, but they can't be expected to put things back at this stage. This activity is a great way to get babies to interact – most babies are even more interested in their neighbour's objects than they are in their own.

3 Let her play with the balls for a while. When she drops one of the balls, pick it up and encourage her to take it from your hand again. Once she has played for a little while, hold out your hand and ask her to give a ball back to you – it's never too early to start working on good manners.

obstacle course

Your baby's mobility is improving rapidly. At eight to nine months of age, she is able to crawl through different sizes of space and is getting good at keeping her head down as she crawls under things. She may be able to crawl onto and even over objects in her path. As she explores, she learns how to control her body in different situations and positions.

You can help encourage these skills by setting up your own baby obstacle course. Use household objects such as cushions, stools and chairs to make obstacles for your baby to crawl around. This type of activity teaches your baby how to move and adapt her body depending on the size of the obstacle. With a little practice, she will be able to cruise through whatever type of course you can invent.

Sensory integration

As your baby starts to crawl she learns to organize and interpret the sensations of gravity and motion. The integration of these sensations with visual information lets her manoeuvre over and around obstacles.

What you will need
Chairs, tables, cushions, pillows – anything that your baby can crawl under, over, or step onto
Your baby's favourite toy

Skills developed
Exploration of space, horizontally and vertically
Whole body control

1 Place your baby in front of a large cushion. Put a favourite toy on top, just out of reach. As your baby reaches for the toy she should lean on the cushion and lift one leg up onto it. She should then transfer her upper body weight onto the cushion and draw up her other knee. Once your baby reaches the toy, put it on the floor so that she learns to climb down and over obstacles, too.

Soccer player

Stand your baby up a little behind a ball such as a soccer or beach ball. Walk him towards the ball and, when he reaches it, help him kick it. Encourage him to take some steps to follow it and kick it again. Repeat the activity with a different-sized ball, such as a tennis ball, to teach him to adjust his kick and the length of his steps.

At this age your baby is gaining more and more control of his lower body, especially his feet. He can now place his feet one after the other and walk with your assistance. At this point, some babies may even stand without any support and attempt to take a few steps on their own.

2 Create a short tunnel for your baby to crawl through by placing a sheet over a chair. Once she gets the hang of this, arrange two or three chairs in a row to make the tunnel longer. To really test your baby, try combining a whole series of obstacles. Use your imagination – the steps shown here are just a start!

peek-a-boo

A baby younger than eight or nine months does not yet fully understand the concept of permanence – as far as an infant is concerned, once someone leaves the room they are gone. But as your baby starts to make more sophisticated connections, her understanding of the way the world around her works will greatly improve.

You can help your baby get used to faces and objects disappearing and reappearing with this simple but lively game. At first, your baby needed you to place an object in front of her in order to visualize it. Now she should start being able to imagine where it might be without having to see it.

What you will need
A bed sheet, scarf or large cloth
A radio or stereo

Skills developed
Awareness of object permanence

Sensory integration

As your baby learns to interpret the world, she uses information received from all her senses. This activity prevents your baby from making use of one sense – her sight – so that she has to rely on others to create a mental image of her surroundings. When you remove the sheet and this image is confirmed, she will realize that things stay the same, even when she can't see them.

1 Sit or lay your baby down on the floor. Take a bed sheet or another large, translucent piece of material and completely cover your baby up in it. Most infants love this game, but if your baby is afraid you can join her under the bed sheet for a few turns before trying her on her own again.

2 On the count of three, lift up the sheet and say "peek-a-boo!" before covering baby up again. Try this a few times – your baby will soon get the hang of the game and may start to anticipate each lift of the sheet with a grin and a chuckle.

3 Hide a radio or a stereo under a big towel in full view of your baby. Start the music playing and she should lift the towel to look for the hidden melody. This game stimulates your baby's short-term visual memory and auditory capabilities.

Older babies

When your baby has grown out of her initial anxiety at being separated from you, you can adapt this game to include an element of hide-and-seek. While she is under the sheet, hide around a corner or behind a table. Let her pull the sheet off herself and call out to her to see if she can work out where you are hiding. Keep a close eye on her, though, to make sure she doesn't get too tangled up or upset.

humpty-dumpty

By this age your baby should be starting to gain full control of her neck, shoulder and lower back muscles. This will help her support and balance her body as she tries to reach for things from a sitting position. When she tried to perform this type of reaching action at six months your baby probably tended to lose her balance and topple over. Now she should be able to rely more on her back and stomach muscles – although she will still put one hand down for support. She may even be able to lift herself back into a sitting position once she has hold of the toy.

Sensory integration

This activity will challenge your baby's understanding of her body in space, improve her upper body control and lower back muscle strength and teach her how to visually examine a toy from many spatial perspectives. The activity requires good motor planning (the ability to imagine the strategy needed to carry out the movement or action) as well as effective vestibular responses such as balance and motor coordination.

What you will need
A rolled up towel or rug big enough to sit your baby on with a leg on each side
Your baby's favourite toy

Skills developed
Lower back muscle control
Reaching action

1 Hold your baby's waist and help her to sit on the roll with one leg on each side. Place a toy on the floor a little in front of her. Assist her as she bends over to pick it up – she should place one hand on the roll, lean forward, and stretch out her other hand to pick up the toy. If her back and stomach muscles are strong enough, she may even lift herself back upright without your help.

2 Place the toy a little further out to the side. To reach it now your baby has to lean right away from the roll. Note how she uses her hands for balance – both hands now need to be on the floor for reaching and grasping the toy, which is not the case when reaching and grabbing from sitting. Keep you hands on her waist in case she topples over.

3 When your baby reaches the object, let her examine it first before asking her to return it to you. This gives her practice at letting go of things. Repeat the activity on the opposite side.

Pot-pourri

Collect together a number of objects with very different textures – use items such as cotton balls, pasta, wood or nuts. Take several small cloth bags of the type used for lavender bags or pot-pourri and place an item inside each one. Let your baby pick up one of the bags and pull out an object. Use the game to teach her basic concepts such as in and out, smooth and rough, hard and soft and big and small. Note her reactions to the different objects.

6

from ten months to one year

Y our baby is fast becoming a toddler. He should now be able to sit,
kneel and perhaps even stand without support – he is acquiring
what a developmental expert might call a more "mature pattern of
postural control".

He is probably crawling all over the house, climbing up and down stairs and
pulling himself up using the furniture. He will stand on his toes to make
himself taller, or on one leg to adjust his balance. Your baby is learning to
make fine adjustments with his posture to maintain stability during his
manoeuvres.

The more variation your baby faces when cruising around your house, the more
skillful he will become in meeting new gross motor challenges and in
developing his problem-solving skills. So don't strive to make the way easier

for him – put a few safe and soft obstacles in his way. Faced by these obstacles your baby learns to create a mental picture of his environment and plan his moves in relation to objects and people.

By this age your baby should also be able to handle new toys and objects very efficiently. He can manipulate them easily, he may experiment with different ways to grip hold of them – he may even start to use objects as tools rather than simply as something to play with or teethe on.

Give him the time to explore and solve simple tasks himself rather than encouraging him to rely on you. It is by exploring the objects around him that he will start to grasp concepts such as in and out, close and open, over and under, and so on. This will help him solve real-life problems – putting different sizes of blocks into the right holes, for example, pulling open drawers, or crawling around or under obstacles. A stimulating, changing environment will encourage him to move, learn and explore.

head over heels

From an early age, children take great delight in bending their bodies backwards. This type of movement keeps the front of the body – the stomach, the chest and the shoulders – open, fluid and relaxed. At the same time it strengthens the back, which will help to maintain good posture.

A ten-month- or year-old baby won't be able to perform backbends by himself, but you can give your little one a feel for the movement by lifting him up and gently flipping him over so that his head is down and his legs are in the air. So long as you perform the exercise slowly and keep the game light and fun, he should enjoy the acrobatic nature of the exercise and the feeling of weightlessness.

Sensory integration

Thrilling sensations are produced as your baby's vestibular system and sense of balance react to changes in his position. You baby uses these sensations, together with visual information, to orient his body in space and work out what action he should take in response to these changes.

What you will need
Just you and your baby

Skills developed
Spinal flexibility
Spatial orientation

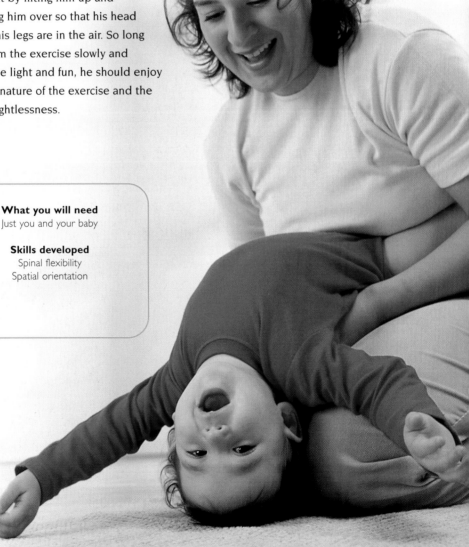

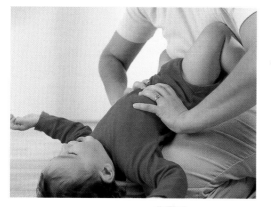

1 Sit back onto your heels and place your baby face up on your lap with his legs around your waist. Hold him with your fingers on his tummy and your thumbs behind his waist. Smile, laugh and talk to him as you do this so he feels relaxed.

2 Very slowly flip your baby's legs over his head. Make sure you give him plenty of time to realize what is happening – you are doing this exercise *with* your baby, not *to* him, and it requires input from him if he is to benefit. He should react to his inverted position by lifting his head and placing his hands down to protect his head.

Bubble time

Try blowing some bubbles for your baby – the slowly floating spheres will fascinate him and stimulate good visual tracking and hand-eye coordination as he tries to grab them. You can buy ready-made solution and a wand for blowing the bubbles in most toy shops. If you prefer, mix your own using 10 parts water, 1 part washing-up liquid, and about ¼ part glycerine.

For a more messy variation on the game, sit your baby in front of a baby bath filled with lukewarm water and lots of baby bubble bath. Put your baby on your knees so that he is high enough to reach in and play with the water while you blow the bubbles over the bath.

baby gym

Your baby loves and needs body contact. You are still one of his favourite "objects" to pull himself up on and one of the most helpful, too, since you can actively respond to and guide him in his attempts. So why not be your baby's gym? He'll get a great workout crawling and climbing over your body.

Putting your baby into a variety of body positions develops the strength, flexibility and coordination needed for free movement in space. As he clambers over you he learns to control his movements and transfer his weight to balance his upper body. The healthy, physical contact will help you both bond, and the physical demands will provide a challenge your baby can face with pleasure.

Sensory integration

The control and coordination your baby needs to orient and manoeuvre his body in space depend on his ability to organize and interpret signals from his proprioceptive, vestibular and visual systems, as well as his awareness of gravity and of his own abilities. Like so much else your baby does at this age, the best way to perfect these skills is simple: practice, practice and more practice.

What you will need
A favourite toy

Skills developed
Mobility and body control

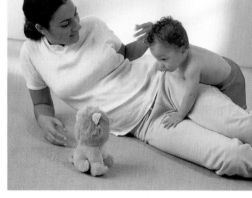

1 Lie sideways on the floor, with your baby behind you. Put a favourite toy in front of you but within his line of sight. Move the toy about to attract your baby's attention and encourage him to climb over you and reach for it.

2 He may use any number of movements to do this, but ideally you want him to rise to a standing position before climbing up and over your hips. As he clambers across you, he should put his hands down onto the floor to bear most of his body's weight and to protect his head. He should then pull himself along to reach the toy. Repeat this activity until your baby can do it without losing his balance.

Making music

Music is a great way to improve your baby's auditory discrimination and rhythm. Half-fill two small, plastic water bottles with uncooked rice or dried beans and glue on the cap so your baby cannot remove it. Let him explore the instrument first, then demonstrate how to shake it and allow him to copy you. Play a recording of an upbeat tune and shake along to the beat. This noisy game also encourages the development of hand-eye coordination and fine motor skills.

round and about

By the end of his first year, your infant should be using his developing cognitive skills to plan and assess his movements. Not only is he capable of overcoming obstacles to reach something or someone he wants, he is also capable of acquiring objects by more indirect means.

In this activity the idea is that your baby moves from sitting to crawling to standing as he progresses around the table and pulls himself up. This will test his ability to change position and approach an object of interest indirectly, by a roundabout route. Let your baby think his approach through for himself. The aim of the activity is not just to get your baby to make the physical movements needed to get hold of the toy – you also want to see how he goes about solving a problem.

What you will need
Coffee table or similar large object
Favourite toy

Skills developed
Mobility and body control
Spatial awareness
Problem solving

Sensory integration
This activity requires good postural reactions, visual ability and motor planning. It teaches your baby to react to situations by assessing, deciding, and acting, and helps him acquire more complex cognitive skills.

1 Sit your baby on the ground around 2 metres (6 feet) from the coffee table. Stand around the opposite side of the table and show him a favourite toy. He should start to crawl towards the toy.

WATCH OUT!

Although your baby is now very mobile, he is still learning how to use his body safely. But while you should make sure he doesn't hit his head or sustain any serious injury, resist the temptation to interfere too much. Your baby needs to experience the odd accident if he is to learn how to calculate risk effectively.

2 Your baby may crawl to the table, pull himself up to a standing position and stretch out his hands to try to reach the toy. When he realizes he can't reach across the table, he will probably take some time to find the way to get to the toy by going around the table. He may lose sight or get confused, but with a little determination he should eventually succeed.

texture touch

Touch forms a vital part of your baby's ability to comprehend his world. He uses his hands to reach out and take hold of objects so he can get a sense of their size, shape and texture. But why should his hands have all the fun?

Sensory integration activities should involve the whole body, your baby will enjoy the chance to provide his feet with some tactile stimulation, too.

This activity gives your baby the chance to experience different types of textures and tactile sensations and at the same time gives him practice walking. Then, sit your baby down so he can reach out using his hands. Through trial and error baby learns to orient his body towards an object, shift his weight in the proper direction and exercise the postural control necessary to execute the reaching action.

Sensory integration
Your baby learns to explore the world around him by simultaneous use of his senses and movement. As he walks over the squares, bends down, picks them up and runs his hands over them, his eyes take in visual information and his hands and feet receive tactile stimulation. He also should by now actively seek out this information by feeling for the textures he finds most intriguing.

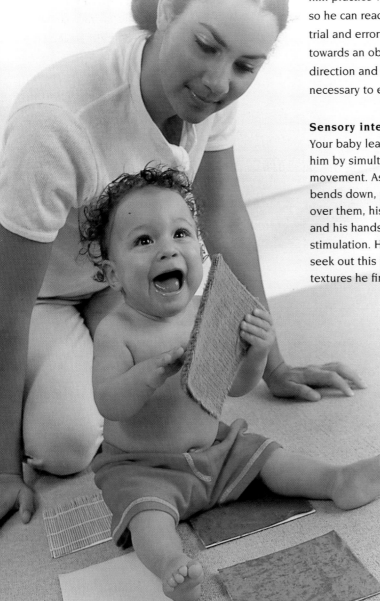

What you will need
Differently textured materials
Thick cardboard

Skills developed
Mobility
Upper body control
Reaching actions

1 Glue pieces of differently textured materials onto squares of thick cardboard, one texture per piece. You could use different fabrics, feathers, pieces of foam, sand, plastic – anything that provides contrast and is safe to walk on. Lay the squares out in a stepping-stones type path across the floor.

2 Stand your baby, barefoot, in front of the first square. Hold his hands at his shoulder height and slightly forward. Guide your baby as he steps onto each square and feels each of the different textures underneath his feet.

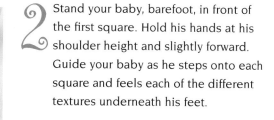

3 Give him time to experience the sensations and to stop or pull his foot away if he wants. Some textures may be so interesting he squats down to explore further.

4 Put your baby on his hands and knees with the squares all around him. This way he learns to reach out and handle objects of various sizes and textures. Talk to him as he feels the squares so he becomes familiar with concepts such as rough, smooth or soft.

Barefoot baby

Don't be in too much of a hurry to cover your baby's feet with his first shoes. Playing barefoot is a great way to develop strength and give him a feel for his environment. Indeed, he probably won't need proper shoes until he's been walking confidently for at least four to six weeks.

you are trapped

By this age your baby should be very mobile – and he will use this mobility to explore and interact with his environment. The goal of this activity is to see how your baby solves a problem. He is on the inside of the "enclosure"; you and the toy are outside – how will he get to you? But you may find that your baby derives as much satisfaction from interacting with the obstacles – ducking underneath the chairs or pushing them apart – as he does from escaping. This activity encourages communication, mobility and problem solving – all excellent skills for your child to develop at this age.

Sensory integration

The ability to change position and move through different obstacles requires good coordination, postural reactions and motor planning from your baby. The more varied the situations that he is placed in, the more practice he gets in integrating and responding to the type of sensory information he will find in day-to-day life.

What you will need
Four kitchen or dining-room chairs
A favourite toy

Skills developed
Problem solving
Mobility and body control
Spatial awareness

1 Set four chairs in a square. You can arrange them with either the backs or the seats facing in – what really matters is that an enclosure is created with space enough inside for your little one to move about. Place your baby inside the square.

2 Attract your baby's attention with a toy then try to get him to climb over, under or between the chairs. Whichever way your baby chooses to escape, be sure to reward him. If he gets too frustrated you should show him a way out, then put him back in the square so he has a chance to try it himself.

Chase me

Your baby is now an expert crawler. He knows how to crawl forwards and backwards, he can move sideways, right and left, and he can quickly readjust his body to suit the situation. It's time for you to get on all fours and chase! But will you be able to keep up with him?

Kneel over your baby and roll a ball far enough in front of you to create a good crawling distance. Your baby should start heading for the ball. When he does, crawl after him and block him with your arms to force him to change direction. Do this in the spirit of fun and he should take up the challenge gleefully.

index

acknowledgments

I would like to dedicate this book to my daughter, Anne-Catherine, with whom I discovered the pleasure of the Prague Parent-Infant Programme (PEKiP); to my son Lukas, who made me realize the importance of bringing this programme to Hong Kong; and to my husband, Andreas, who has supported me in all my projects.

I would like to thank Virginia Sheridan for interpreting the work I do and for bringing her writing skills to this special project – I am grateful for her excellent work. I owe much gratitude to Rachel Aris, who attended my classes with her daughter Hannah, read my book, edited it brilliantly, and encouraged me to present it to Carroll & Brown. Additional thanks to Amy Carroll, to Tom Broder for the final editing work, and to all of the beautiful models, big and small.

Carroll & Brown would like to thank:
Photographic assistant **David Yems**
Hair and make-up **Kathinka** at Joy Goodman

And a special thanks to our mums/dads and babies:
Harriet and Jasmine, Fiona and Sadie, Deborah and Emily, Kaya and Jolie, Shiela and Connor, Sandrine and Mila, Greta and Naomi, Tamar and Mio, Ayiesha and Morgan, Samantha and Luca, Laura and Mala, Sly and Jermaine, Jayne and Dalia, Josephine and Jed, Sophy and Lily, Sarah and Ben, Mary-Ann and Samuel, Evie and Anthony, Dagmar and Nora, Caroline and Isabelle, Claire and Luca, Leo and Teague, Kareen and Antwan